Life Destiny

By: Steve Ryan

©Copyright 2014 by Steve Ryan
Life Destiny
ISBN-13: 978-0692269176 (Steve Ryan)
ISBN-10: 0692269177
Published by: Steve Ryan Publishing
Cover Design By: Douglas Garnett

Table of Contents

Introduction 6

Chapter 1 - Turning Lemons into Lemonade 7

The Struggle 9
A Brand New Day 12
I Will Not Be Defined By A Moment 13
I Am Finally Liberated 14
Listen To Your Courage 16
The Unbreakable Journey 17
Look Inside Your Mental Sea 19
When I Look In The Mirror 20
Real Time 21
The Timid Approach 22
When Everything Seems Lost 23
The Power Of Enlightenment 24
Real Clarity 25

Chapter 2 – Ticked Off 27

Shut Up 29
Furious, Angry, Betrayed 31
Trusting People 33
A Frustrating Day 34
The Snake 35
Complexity 37
Why Are You So Lazy? 38
You Arrogant Fool 39
How Dare You? 40
Family Betrayal 42

Is This The End Of Our Friendship?...44
Your Attitude Sucks..45
The Murder Of My Friend 46
Chapter 3 – Letting Life Flow...48
Let Nature Take Its Course 49
Like The Ants, We March Everyday..51
Nature 52
Why Drain My Energy?..53
I Decided To Let Go 54
Insanity Bites 56
Deep Sea Swim..57
Her Message Before She Passed 58
Walk With Nature 60
Chapter 4 - Depression 62
Dark History..64
Overdose 66
Down 69
Medication 70
Another Hard Day..71
Feelings Of Vanity 72
I Am So Unhappy Right Now 74
Help Me 76
Here I Am Again 77
How Long?...79
Chapter 5 – What Does Life Mean?..81
Thoughts On A Cold Day..82
This Throbbing Headache 83
The True Purpose Of Life 85

This Little Mouse 87
The Serene Amazement 88
The Three Realities 89
Uncertainty 92
Want More 93
The Real Possession 94
The Foolish Deceiver 95
A New Era 97
The Lesson From The Fishermen 99
Conclusion **101**

Introduction

Life Destiny is a very interesting concept. It's a question that people often ask themselves. I've even asked myself questions about my own Life Destiny. What is my purpose here? Where is my life heading? Why do people treat me this way? Why did it happen to me? What is the meaning of it all? When it comes to Life Destiny, the questions are endless.

This book will take you through a journey through some of the different stages of Life Destiny. The voyage of this book starts off with the inspiring chapter of "Turning Lemons into Lemonade." Then we will venture into the anger land of "Ticked Off." After that, we will calm down, breathe and we'll arrive at "Letting Life Flow." After we are flowing for some time, we will be pulled into the sea of "Depression." Once we survive this, we will finally arrive at the last chapter of this book, "What Does Life Mean?"

The up and down cycles of life have touched us all at some point in our lives. It's like a roller coaster ride that's unpredictable. I've experienced this before. One minute my life was going great and then all of a sudden, an obstacle was thrown my way. During those times, I have asked myself these questions. What do I do? How do I handle it? How have others handled it? In some cases, knowing other people's experiences with similar situations can bring clarity. This has helped me with some of my life decisions. Obstacles will come. That's a fact. It's not a matter of if; it's a matter of when. The outcome can be affected by the decision of how it is managed. We will explore these things and more throughout this book. So fasten your seatbelt and enjoy the ride through this book of Life Destiny.

Chapter 1

Turning Lemons into Lemonade

Our first stop is Turning Lemons into Lemonade. That is the perfect title for this chapter. Have you ever had those "fight or flight" moments in your life? These are the moments in which a problem is thrown across your path and you're faced with making a decision on how to handle it. When I've come across these situations, there were several questions that crossed my mind. Do I run from the problem? Do I ignore it and hope it goes away? Do I stand up and face the problem head on and power through it? What do I do?

This chapter focuses more on standing up to the problem and overcoming it. There are more to these poems than simply expressing inspiration. These poems are realistic and provide insight while entertaining and inspiring at the same time. Some of these poems reflect situations that I've personally experienced and others reflect situations that I've seen others experience. This realistic poetic expression will help you better connect and relate to the message behind the poems.

Turning Lemons into Lemonade is one of my favorite concepts in life. It is another form of overcoming obstacles and triumphing over trials and tribulations. I relate to this very well based on my own life experiences. I'm a huge believer in positive manifestation followed by taking action.
When I'm faced with an obstacle, my normal course of action is to confront it head on with a determined mindset to overcome it. There are also other courses of actions that can be taken as well depending on the circumstances.

One weapon that can be used to overcome obstacles is having the right mindset. This is what I've used in my methods over time. I keep a winning attitude. I don't expect life to be perfect, however, I don't believe in letting problems consume me. Figuratively speaking, I put on my boxing gloves and I fight my problems until they are out of my way. This attitude makes it easier to keep my determination to overcome obstacles.

I'm sure you've heard many stories of what different people have gone through to achieve success in their lives. I've experienced the same in my own life. It was not easy reaching success and being successful does not eliminate problems. This is why I have to remind myself at times to continue to keep a positive mindset regardless of what speed bumps come along my path.

The collection of poems in this chapter shows strength in the face of adversity. It's something that most people will be able to connect to and be empowered by. These poems are down to earth and relatable regardless of your background. It's time for you to be inspired like I am. Feel the energy of my words. Feel the inspiration as you overcome your obstacles. This is our time to turn "Lemons into Lemonade."

The Struggle

The struggle seem never ending

Does it have to be this hard to survive?

Why is it so difficult to succeed?

Every time I turn around, another problem finds its way to me

I keep coming across discouraging predicaments

Was this the harvest of something that I did in my past?

I work so hard but nothing gives in

How much longer is this going to last?

All of the pressure on me is very taxing

Although my outside appearance indicate the opposite

My inside is one that is on the verge of collapsing

I want to have hope, but does hope even exist?

At what point will this hardship end?

I have to find a way to get through it

What will it take for my overcoming to begin?

I need an answer, I feel so clueless

I think of the future and I say to myself

How will my life be in a few years?

Will my struggle be the same?
I don't want it to exist
My decision has been made
I'm choosing to overcome it

I search and I search within myself for my will
I need it to survive all battles that are coming my way
When can I live my life?
I need some worry free days

The story of my struggle
Drives me insane
I can't take it anymore
Things have to change

I'm going to change my mindset
I will stand up and fight
It's pointless for me to stay upset
When I have a vision of my future in plain sight

No more, no more, no more
This is what I will say
To any negative influences that attack me
Nothing will take my resolve away

I will not continue to struggle

I will break these chains, one circumstance at a time

When things appear to be near their end

That's when I'll know that my breakthrough will begin

I will enjoy my struggle free mind

A Brand New Day

I just woke up to the morning sun
The light shines on my eyes
I'm going to force myself out of bed
The sunlight has inspired me to rise
Today is a brand new day
I had a very long night
There are so many thoughts in my brain
Depression has taken over my sight

I've reached a point of unhappiness
It's been hard for me to rest
I've plunged into a deep depression
This is the reality that I've met
Why do obstacles keep coming my way?
When one is gone, another takes its place
Hello universe, tell me what is going on
I need a break, have I done something wrong?

The pressure is so much
It's very hard to breathe
I feel like this world is designed
To keep us all in need
Life doesn't have to be this way
I'm saying this to myself within
I'm deciding that on this brand new day
I am not going to give in

I will stand up and do the best I can
These are my new thoughts
I'm constructing a new plan
It's time for me to leave depression land

I Will Not Be Defined By A Moment

I will not be defined by a moment
This moment is just a second in time
This won't knock me from my direction
Even through this negative, my plans will stay alive

I've learned what things to do
When I feel stagnant and stuck
I will chip away through any obstacle's clay
I will keep persisting and create my own luck

I've learned to feel my vibrations
I pay attention to how my energy flows
When I feel trapped and suffocated
I let this feeling go

It wasn't easy to put this into practice
Especially when I've had bad habits
Sometimes I would stay inside of my head
I became a victim to my own circumstance

After being down so long
I finally realized the truth
I can't feel sorry for myself
There are things that I can do

I won't stay trapped
I will kick the door open
My life won't be defined
By this horrible moment

I Am Finally Liberated

This morning I was liberated

I was freed from my own mental suppression

It took a lot of pain to make me realize

That I was enslaved to my own mentality

I thought badly about myself

There was so much negativity

I gave up

I had no energy left to work on my dreams

I sabotaged relationships

The real issue resided within me

It wasn't other people's fault

I had a warped view of reality

I was holding myself back from achieving

I blamed others too long

When I should have looked at myself

I was in the wrong

But now that I have lived
I have truly learned
I am finally freed from my voluntary suppression
I can see the rising sun

I have decided to stand up against negativity
I won't live for what I think other people want to see
This is what enslaved my mentality
My mindset matched what others wanted it to be

Some people see me as being shy and a loner
But that's not me
Some people picture me as very friendly and sociable
But that's not me

Some people picture me as being scared and timid
That's definitely not me
I am simply a free flowing spirit
I will be however I will be

I am ready to be liberated and to be free
I will start again to work toward my dreams
This is my time to regain focus
I'm no longer mentally enslaved and I can finally see

Listen To Your Courage

You have a beautiful spirit
I love your beautiful smile
Your energy is big enough
To go for thousands of miles

You are so uplifting
I can sense you're positive and giving
You even make a depressed person
Find a reason for living

Think about these thoughts
When you are feeling worthless
You inspire me to not have doubts
You have so much courage

Resist that negative energy
Don't let it win at convincing
I've been through what you're feeling
Your presence has energetic healing

When you're feeling down and out
And fear is circling around
You have to unleash your instincts within
And fight that battle until you win

It's time to listen to your courage

The Unbreakable Journey

It's truly unimaginable
Of what a negative image could mean
It's truly indescribable
Of what revealing the truth would bring
If only everyone knew
Of the truth really inside
It's a world full of fear and discourage
And contempt to the depths inside

Everyone looks up to me
As a man that can get the job done
If only they knew how rough it is
When my money is next to none
I hold my head up and keep my chin high
As I encourage everyone to have success
I look up above and sing to the sky
And say I must I must I must survive

How much pressure can I really take?
Before I break my peace
How many obstacles must I cross?
Before reaching the heavenly scene
Success can be so hard to reach
Even when it's only a touch away
And freedom is not what freedom means
Because I'm locked to commitments in chains

So I continue to play the role
Of this successful image filled with wealth
But inside I am about to lose my mind
And I've neglected to take care of my health
So I decide to take a firm approach
I decided to not give in
And finally I reached true success
I finally can say I win

I'm glad that I didn't give up
Now my image matches my wealth
I'm finally enjoying the fruits of my labor
And I'm taking care of myself
Right when I was about to give up
My journey left its rocky road
And now it was worth all that I've been through
Now my path is paved with gold

I'm so glad that I didn't break away
I stayed on the path that I had laid
And even when trials would bring me down
I stood up every time I hit the ground
And now I am truly a real success
And I've made some great progress
This was all because I didn't give in
My journey was unbreakable, yes I win

Look Inside Your Mental Sea

You are not a failure
You did the best that you can
Sometimes trials create a way
To achieve your master plan

Don't worry if it's something you can't see
You won't understand every step of your path
But in the end, history tells the same tale
Your rough journey doesn't make your destination fail

I know you are tired of hearing
People telling you to stay strong
But when you look at the big picture
You are not alone

We all go through trials and tribulations
That's just the way of life
It's all part of the world's equation
Success adds up from sacrifice

It's time to let go of "I can't" thoughts
Those make you stay on hold
It's time for you to have power and release
Just look inside your mental sea

When I Look In The Mirror

I'm thinking about surrendering
Giving in to my circumstance
It seems as if every time I turn around
Nothing seems to be working

I told myself this morning
That I am going to have a good day
But it seem like every single hour
Bad news is hitting me in the face

I looked into the mirror
Pondering and asking myself why
What can I do to change things?
What do I need to sacrifice?

This burden upon me is making me frown
What will it take to overcome these trials?
The past just seems to not let me forget
Some of my decisions I've grown to regret

I looked into the mirror
I see who I am today
Most of my problems from the past
Came from me giving so much, even my last

It's a sad situation to come to this conclusion
That helping people is not a good solution
Now my focus must be on me
This is now my new reality

Real Time

I have new way of thinking
My understanding is expanding over time
Inside a new light is shining
The old frustration is escaping from my mind
All of my dark side is leaving
Procrastinating is vacating from my style
In place a new sun is rising
And condemnation is evaporating to the sky

I have a new way of breathing
The old pollution is revoluting from my eye
Now lies a new kind of seeing
My appreciation is elevating to a high
I feel a new way of feeling
My past emotion is diverting to the side
I'm grateful for my mental healing
Now my confusion is eluding from my mind

I just want to stay in real time
I'm going to move forward
I won't hit rewind
I don't want get stuck by looking behind
I'm going to live my life
I won't hit rewind
I don't want to stop
I don't want to pause
I just want to live each day and live each minute
I want to make each moment count in real time

The Timid Approach

I think you are nice and sweet
You have a real beauty inside
It's time let go of your past
So that your beauty inside can shine

For when you hold onto that dark history
You'll never finish crossing your mental seas
You must see yourself as great
And not let your good be overridden with bad

It's time for you to gain some strength
You're too easy for others to persuade
So I will pray for your strength
Your mind needs to be aware
You're too compassionate, you overly care

In the past you've been misused
Over and a thousand times over again
You let people give you so much abuse
Your timid approach holds you down within

When Everything Seems Lost

When everything seems lost
And seem so far away
This is my time to buckle down
I will overcome this today

I will celebrate my life
I choose to be grateful
I won't let my sacrifice
Cause me not to be thankful

I remember reaching an all-time low
I received blow after blow
Everything seemed lost to me
And no, this wasn't a dream

I decided not let this phase
Dictate my life's direction
I am going to stand up
And fight until I reach satisfaction

I won't be enslaved
To a losing mentality
I will be victorious this day
There will be peace inside of me

The Power of Enlightenment

I will listen to my inner voice
I can hear those thoughts
My spirit is trying to guide me
So that I will know the truth from the false

I have been enlightened
On the truth that I need to see
And now it's my time
I will get rid of negativity

I can do anything in my life
That I want to do
I will let my spirit guide me
And I'll find my way to my truth

I am destined for great things
And it's time to take control
I will get rid of all my demons
They will not place my life on hold

I will overcome my past
My pain will no longer last
It's time to embrace a new beginning
I can feel my mind, now it's transcending

I will stay positive and stay strong
I know that I'm not alone
This is the real truth to be told
My enlightenment is now known

Real Clarity

I have achieved real clarity today
Although these thoughts have hit my mind
Challenges will remain along my way
I know inside the steps that I need to take
It doesn't make it easier to get through each day
At least I can have a good positive start
That's better than being stuck in time like art

I must take one day at a time
I can be happy and unwind
I will surround myself with good thoughts and I won't stress
I have to ensure that I survive my own emotional mess
Life doesn't have to be so difficult
It doesn't have to be so hard
It's all about managing the things that make up who we are

I hope I won't cave in to my endless sacrifice
It's my goal to wake up without stress
I can achieve letting go of my negative past
And use it as a positive forward learning experience
I want to be able to avoid great sadness
It's possible to achieve the ultimate satisfaction
Everything will be ok within me

There have been enough emotions of being depressed
It's a fight each step so that happiness isn't suppressed
This spirit of resignation will not have its way
I am a warrior and I will take charge and have my say
Although it may sound a little cliché
But hey, cliché can be good, although sometimes it's bad
It's all in what you make of it, it not always so sad

This is the real clarity that I have achieved
I will start today by looking at this like a need
Applying this clarity will be a little hard
But hard doesn't mean impossible
The reward is great by far
This is a war that I will win
My clarity gives me strength on which I can depend

Chapter 2 - Ticked Off

What causes you to get ticked off? Is it the way someone talks to you? Is it something that someone does to you? Perhaps it's a life situation like a financial issue or some other problem. Avoiding frustration can be challenging to accomplish at times.

One of the top things that have frustrated me in the past was being betrayed. Have you ever been betrayed by someone? Or perhaps you thought someone's agenda was sincere and it turned out to be deceit. The reason why this is at the top of my list is because I am a very loyal person by nature.

My natural personality causes me to be compassionate and giving to people in general. When someone enters into my circle with bad intentions, this hits me to my core. If it is someone close to me like a family member or close friend, this is equivalent to someone taking a dagger and stabbing me in the heart.

I experienced this with a family member who stole from me and they were dishonest in a major way. They violated my trust in every way and felt no remorse whatsoever. This was hurtful and it angered me. It took me time to recover from this. I was close to this family member. I didn't know who I could trust after that happened.

That betrayal pushed me to a point in my life in which I started to have my walls up tremendously. I would withdraw from people close to me and keep them at a distance. I had to correct myself and return back to my natural trusting nature with a certain adjustment. I learned how to set better boundaries without changing who I am as a person. Regardless of someone else's intentions, I won't allow them to hurt me. I chose not to let that anger linger in my energy.

There are many other types of situations that make people ticked off. This chapter dives into some diverse situations that cause frustration. You will feel the message in some of these poems as if it was your own. They cover a broad range of frustrating situations. Welcome to the chapter, "Ticked Off."

Shut Up

Shut up
Why do you speak?
The words that floweth out of your mouth
Means the same as defecation to me

Shut up
I must tell you
That if you only listen
You'll find what you're looking for

Just shut up!!
Please hear me out
I'm trying to show you
The best way out

You think that you have all the answers
You're finding out that you really don't know
It's because your mouth is literally never closed
And you wonder why life never changes I suppose

So shut up!!
Do you think you are wise?
If you knew all of the answers
Then why are you not content inside?

If you only learn when to speak
Then my friend, everything will be
Just as you want it to be
You'll find your fulfilling destiny

But you never close your mouth
Instead you always close your ears
As if you are the true wise man
That roams the earth free and clear

So if you want to find
What you are really looking for
Then I suggest that you begin
By taming that ignorance within

So SHUT UP!

Furious, angry, betrayed

Furious, angry, betrayed
Those three words described how I felt
After I tried to help someone
They took my kindness and hit me below the belt

Beneath their big smile
There was a pile of treason
Regardless of me giving them good
Evil became their season

I kept up my end of the bargain
They received what they were promised
I help their dream come true
While at the same time I was being used

Then suddenly their hopes and fears collided
Their past transgressions caught up from behind them
This was their history before they met me
"What goes around, comes around", was now reality

So instead of being mature
And accepting the destined truth
They played the victim
They blamed me too

How could they do this?
I always bent over backwards
I was loyal to a fault
And I was stabbed with a dagger

Had I known the end results
I would not have involved myself so deep
Now I'm still feeling anger
I must find a way to pacify the inward me

For I hear these words of wisdom
That tells me to forgive but not forget
I can't allow what happened
To change the way I am

Today I am still so furious
My insides are melting with anger
I remember hearing their deceitful lies
I witnessed their wrongful betrayal

I was utterly disgusted
When I discovered their intentions
They had plans to destroy me
However fate saved me with an intervention

I will never forget
Feeling furious, anger and betrayed

Trusting People

I can't believe you violated my trust
How could you do this to me?
I thought you were my close friend
But now you're my worst enemy

I won't harbor ill feelings inside
I believe in karma's truth
You can run and hide
But it will come and find you

You were great at pretending
Showing compassion and care
While you were plotting and planning
I must admit you fooled me well

You were very clever
With actions that mirror deceit
You entered my world bearing gifts
When your true intent was to bring misery

This makes it hard to trust people
When their agenda is unclear
Will they be good or evil?
Only time will tell what will appear

A Frustrating Day

I am having a frustrating day
My car is stuck
And my money is misplaced

It's hard to pay attention
I feel scattered in my mind
I refuse to start panicking

I'm in danger if I stay here inside
I'm in the middle of the road
The oncoming traffic might collide

I open the door and the rain starts to fall
The temperature is dropping
Night is starting to call

My hands are cold
My feet are wet
I'm starting to have so much regret

My cell charge is running low
I'm stranded on the side of the road
I just want to go home

Why did this happen today?
I'm right in the middle of change
My anger increases in every way

I would love to fly away
I feel helpless, helpless, help-less
This is a frustrating day

The Snake

I see a snake with yellow piercing eyes
Its tongue is made of double edge forks
With teeth made of deceitful ivory
It has an outside that displays false gold

This snake used to be my friend
We met through tons of laughter
It came to me offering help, joy and life edification
But yet it brought pain, misery, heartache

The snake's plan was to destroy my destiny?
Am I in a dream in which I am to awake?
I think it's time to battle this snake
To face it head to head

Mind to mind
Strength to strength
I will not be afraid
I will have honor, valor and courage

This snake is a master with words
It uses this gift to battle me
I must be strong and alert
I need my strength for a victory

This snake will use obstacles
This is the weapon it sends
I create my own destiny
I refuse to give in

I won't lose to this snake
My strategy has become clear
My plan is to beat it at its game
I can do this, I won't have fear

It's better to keep your enemies close
This is the way to learn their plans
At least I recognized the snake in time
This is the first step towards my win

Complexity

Why is the human mind so complex?
It's impossible to be tamed
Our tongue is more powerful than any bomb
It's caused death upon millions

Deceit comes smooth as honey
Tasting sweet but causing stomach aches.
It's hard to truly understand
The complexity of the human mind

The best times of my life appeared after hurt
It seems as if good and bad are twins
One was born right after the other
Bad competes with everything good creates

Betrayal is the worst form of deceit
When I thought I was living in happiness
Deceit took a knife
And it sliced my arm open

As the blood flowed out
I cried stop, it hurts.
Blood that has flowed out can't be returned
The pain was left behind for an infinite period

I ask myself in my mind
Is this a dream?
I can't believe this is true
One of a million chances fell on me

Why Are You So Lazy?

Why are you so lazy?
I never will understand
You complain and complain
You say that you never can win

Do you wonder why life is this way?
You're not the only person with hardships
But you ignore yours
You try to avoid it

You walk through life with your mind asleep
And your common sense is broken in two
I don't feel sorry for you
Your objective in life is to see who you can use

You vent about staying at the same level
Why are you surprised?
If you don't work at making changes
What other results can you expect to arise?

If you don't get things together
This will be the story of your life
Being lazy is not the answer
There's no need to keep asking why

You Arrogant Fool

You are a fool
How dare you act so arrogant?
You're not being cool
How dare you act so rude?

I have been there for you
Why are you so condescending?
I can't believe what I'm hearing
You are good at offending

I received your urgent message
I thought you were in distress
But once again you played the victim
Why don't you give it a rest?

It seems as if you toy with me
You try to play with my mind
Wow, you're full of deceit
Narcissism is your real treat

I'm putting out an olive branch
To try to mend the fences
But now you're making me regret
You're back to bad intentions

The sad part to it all
Is that you don't really care
Your arrogance fits you very well
In your mind, there's no conscience there

How Dare You?

How dare you say what you said to me?
You think you can talk to me that way?
My frustration inside is ready to release
You're the boiling point of my day

The first issue that I have with you
Is your condescending tone
You just continue to go on and on
Grrrr, just leave me alone

What is your problem?
Tell me, what is your deal?
I don't get why you are acting this way
Will you listen to my appeal?

I'm really trying not to hate you
But you are pushing me to that point
What has gotten into you?
Do you need to go smoke a joint?

I'm not advocating you to do this
But something has got to give
You need a better way to deal with your issues
I'm not your therapist, let's get real

How dare you disrespect me?
You narcissistic fool
You better tread carefully
You're about to get schooled

I'm going to put you in your place
This will be the last time
There is no coming back from this
I will accept no apologies in my mind

You can't go on treating people this way
This isn't the way to be
You have to be aware of what you say
How dare you talk like this to me?

I am done with you
Believe me this is real
I'm cutting you off, there's no more talk
You don't exist to me, here's my goodbye seal

Family Betrayal

Have you ever felt ripped apart?
Like someone threw stones at your heart
That's how I felt
When I was betrayed by someone in my family

I could not believe this when it happened
Why did they do this to me?
I supported them
Who can you trust if you can't trust family?

I gave them all that I had
They squeezed the life out of me
It wouldn't have felt so bad
If betrayal wasn't part of the scene

My frustration grows profusely
I feel like a madman
This situation is getting to my head
I'm going to need a cat scan

Betrayal is like a poison
It works like a disease
Once it infects your trust
The heartbreak will make you bleed

Maybe there's a cure
A way to rebuild trust
I'm too hesitant to take that chance
I have to cut you off, I have to, I must

Once you betrayed me
Our relationship was through
We are no longer family
My kindness will not be abused

Do you think I'm stupid?
I know I'm not wrong
You're full of dishonesty
We will never get along

I tried to listen to reason
The things that people say
They say trust your family no matter what
How can this be true when they betray?

I'm so torn
It's hard to know what to do
I was nice by nature when I was born
But now I feel like a fool

Being betrayed by a family member
There is no greater deceit
The word trust don't exist
Our bond is dead to me

Is This The End Of Our Friendship?

You say that we are friends
But that doubt is starting within
I'm starting to see the signs
That maybe our friendship should end

I'm not sure why these signs came
The bond between us isn't the same
I can't explain this internal separation
All I know is that I'm not enjoying our conversations

All of a sudden you annoy me
With every word that you speak
Is it that my eyes are now able to see?
All of your envy, hate and jealousy

Am I feeling this way just in this moment?
Or is this a feeling that is more permanent?
I'm tired of our struggle growing more and more
Why is it that we always have a mental tug of war?

Even through all of this, I don't hate you
I just think that I need some space from you
I need a chance to clear my head
So that I can make a clear decision instead

I don't know if this feeling is just this second
Or if it's something that I may end up regretting
But right now I just don't trust you
I can't explain it and this feeling isn't new

Your Attitude Sucks

Why do you have an attitude?
It really sucks
Your expression is very mean on your face
You love giving me dirty looks

You roll your eyes
You shake your head
What is your reason?
Are you upset with something I've said?

The only problem with that reason
Is that I haven't said anything
I guess we've entered attitude season
I will avoid you at all costs today

Your energy is so draining
I can't wait to go home
I think you're really crazy
Maybe that's why you're alone

I refuse to keep doing this
You're really pissing me off
I don't mind a debate if there's a real reason
But you're dramatic and stubborn like a rock

Oh you're attitude it sucks
I am making it official this day
Stay as far away from me as possible
This is the last thing you will hear me say

The Murder Of My Friend

I called your name
I reached out to embrace
You moved so far away
But our friendship remain

You never made me feel alone
It's nice to know that someone cared
You were my family even through despair
You were there for me, when no one else was there

How could life be so wrong?
So many questions left unsolved
You were here with us one minute
And then you were killed in just an instant

Your life was so unfinished
How could someone be so cold?
To cross that limit
And leave your loved ones alone

I remember days
You made me smile
You knew what to say
To bring laughter around

And when we used to talk on the phone
You inspired me to press on
You gave me courage and strength
Now you're gone and things won't be the same

I was sad for a while
And now I'm just mad
You didn't do anything to deserve
The circumstances that you had

I still don't understand
Why would someone kill you?
Why would they stick a knife in you?
How could they be so cruel?

Words can't describe my enragement
You were truly a good person
There was no staging in your behavior
Maybe you were too trusting

I don't understand what happened
 Why did you have to leave this world so soon?
I wish I could get my hands on your killer
If it was legal, I would enforce the eye for an eye rule

Chapter 3 - Letting Life Flow

Have you ever heard of the saying "carpe diem?" It means seize the day. Live in the present moment. Have you ever heard of "que sera, sera"? That phrase means, what will be, will be. I'm a big fan of these sayings. I'm a creative person by nature and I love those times when I can be in the moment. Other times life requires me to structure and plan things. I am flexible enough to do this. What about you? What kind of person are you? Do you let your life flow or are you a super planner?

Different people have different rhythms when it comes to how they live their lives. Letting life flow doesn't necessarily mean to take it easy all the time. The flow of life is like a river. It bends and turns. There are even moments that it splashes against rocks and other moments that it flows smoothly downstream. This is the way life is.

This chapter explores the different parts of the river of life. Have you ever had a time that you had to let go of control? These are moments in which you allow things to just be however they are. What about those other moments in which you have to take control and take action? All of these things are the flow of life. The poems in this chapter will close out this journey on the river of life. Now we have arrived at the river of "Letting Life Flow."

Let Nature Take Its Course

It's time to let go
Today I'll be free
This is the right time
To relax and breathe
There's so many times
That I get in my own way
Instead of staying natural
I force things and it causes delays

I'm guilty of overthinking
Analyzing details to the core
But as soon as I back off
All the answers begin to pour
I guess I must be insane
Why do I expect things to change?
It's obvious I haven't learned my lesson
I keep repeating the same mistakes

I'm going against evolution
I keep myself in confusion
When the answer is a simple solution
If I go with the flow, I'll have a good conclusion

I look at the birds and the bees

The flowers and the trees

They all seem so free

They just let things be

The spirit of the earth speaks

It corrects the rights and wrongs

That's the pure essence of balance

That's why there are storms

I relate to the balance of nature

That's the story of my life

One day I'm on cloud nine

And the next moment is full of sacrifice

I've decided to accept this flow of life

I won't let the waves stress me inside

One minute it's up, the next minute it's down

It only takes one second between a smile and a frown

My soul has spoken with its voice

I've listened now and I'm making a choice

I refuse to panic, I won't hear that noise

I will let go and let nature take its course

Like The Ants, We March Everyday

Like the ants, we march everyday

Same task, different day

Sometimes hope seems only a reach away

Other times, a hopeless future appears to stay

I ask myself, what is the meaning of life?

Why does life seem like it is on repeat?

I feel like I'm inside of a vacuum

There is no escape

This is how life can seem from day to day

But like the ants, we keep marching on

I sit here and think, what's our common goal?

As I'm here contemplating, I wonder

Are some people more favoured than others?

When we strip down our outside, we all are one in the same.

We are the same, part of the masses.

I sit here on this train, just listening

On one end there are people talking nice

On the other, there are people being hateful

What divides the masses? What makes our beliefs true?

I feel eyes on me as I write

Like the ants, we march every day

Nature

I like to go outside in the morning for fresh air
It's perfect for meditation out there
Oh I can hear nature as I breathe
It's whispering through the trees
The wind is massaging me with its touch
It's very gentle and it's not too much
The birds are singing and chirping their songs
This is so peaceful, it goes on so long
Reality is speaking, time is going by
It's almost time to return to life and say goodbye
My spirit has left my body, it hasn't returned
It's floating around and enjoying the air
It's ready to re-enter, I can feel it coming near
I've awaken my senses from the deep atmosphere
Meditating with nature is like being out of body
My hearing is clear and my vision isn't cloudy
My mind is at peace and I'm feeling at ease
I've bonded with nature under this tree

<u>Why Drain My Energy?</u>

I'm not going to drain my energy

I will stay calm and stay clear

I want to keep in line with synergy

I want all of my worries to disappear

When I get around you

You talk way too much

It's like you go on and on

And complain about the world and such

I'm not saying people can't talk

But whoa, can we have some balance

I just want some carpe deim

Our conversations doesn't have to be a challenge

I just want things to flow smoothly

I really value my peace

Let's just relax and take it easy

And let things be however they will be

I Decided To Let Go

I allowed anger to build up inside
I was consumed with worry
All these thoughts about how things will happen
It ate me alive, it started so early

What can I do to fix my problems?
How can I make them go away?
These were part of my thoughts
That I experienced heavily today

I felt blocked inside
I couldn't unwind
I tried everything under the son
To help me clear my mind

Nothing worked for me
I was full of anxiety
But one day it occurred to me
That the answer wasn't hiding

In the face of problems

I was making a complicated scene

I had to let up

And give things room to breathe

And as soon as I tried this

I saw results immediately show

And that's when I decided

It's time to let things go

Insanity Bites

You try the same thing over and over
Now you're frustrated that it's not different results
What did you expect would be different?
Insanity is creeping into your home

I'm not saying there's anything wrong with trying
But at least change your approach
It's no used to complaining
All I hear is venting from your throat

Instead of trying to force things
Maybe you should try on a different coat
How about a more natural way?
It could give you different results

But I guess you enjoy the same cycle
Maybe it's your reality high
It's time to be neutral and not spiteful
Relax and tell your insanity goodbye

Deep Sea Swim

I recently went swimming
It was a way to make my head clear
I remember stroking wave by wave
And I decided to dive without gear

I connected with the ocean
Swimming with the fish underneath
When I'm in the deep sea
Nothing in this world bothers me

I'm back stroking in the water
Oh it feels so good
I don't want to leave this place
I'll just eat some fish if I want some food

Whenever life throws me lemons
I'll just make lemonade
I'll remind myself about the ocean
This deep sea swim won't fade

Her Message Before She Passed

Grandma was in pain

I sat beside her bed trying not to cry

She said son

Please just close your eyes

Don't worry

My future is secure

I'm in no hurry

To ask for a cancer cure

There's no reason

For you to feel hurt inside

I'm happy where I'm going

There shouldn't be tears in your eyes

I won't feel pain

I won't feel duress

I won't feel tired any longer

My spirit will be at its best

So don't worry

Just focus on your rest

I've enjoyed my time in this world

I've had good times and some bad

But one thing that I can say

Is that I have no regret

I think about my treasures

That's in another world

And there's much pleasure

In knowing you will someday learn

This was the message

That my Grandma said

Don't worry Grandma

Your message was received in my head

Walk With Nature

It's such a beautiful day
As I walk pass these trees
The air is very clean
As I smell the smell of nature
As I walk these trails
I can see a picture of myself
My life has suddenly changed
I feel so great

I see that little fly
It reminds me of my past
Of a time when I used to cry
Oh those memories fade so fast
It's amazing
Of the things you see
When you take a walk on the trail
And spend time with nature itself

It's a beautiful day
Special in every way
I feel I will have a good future
I can envision where it will lead

I'm glad I took time
To realize the faith inside of me
This awesome day lets me unwind

I see refreshing memories
Nature is having its way
I love sitting by this stream
I lean back on the grass and lay
The sun is shining up above
The warm heat hits my face
I feel so great, my mind is clear
All of my negative thoughts are erased

Chapter 4 - Depression

Have you ever been depressed? Or have you had a depressed moment? Depression is a very touchy subject. It's one of those emotions that are hard for some people to admit they have. I am guilty of this as well. I'm so used to being positive minded and speaking positive things. I am very tight lipped about my moments of depression. People around me didn't know when I've been depressed in the past. I would still have a smile on my face on the outside.

I believe that depression is more common than we think. Some people experience it at different intensities and frequencies than others. There are so many commercials for depression medication out there. Why is that? Do a large percentage of people suffer from depression? Is this why there are so many advertisements?

I have had my own learning experience from past depression. I used to run from it, ignore it and pretend it didn't exist. I would stay active and do anything in the world to avoid facing the issues that caused my depression. I continued this until one day it caught up with me. Here is what happened.

One of my good friends was murdered some time ago. It was an unfortunate and traumatic incident. I chose to ignore the pain from this loss. I wouldn't even let myself cry. I stayed active and busy as long as I could for weeks. I would rarely sleep at the time. I did not want to talk about what happened. I just pretended it didn't happen.

Finally one day, it all came crashing down. My body was exhausted but yet I could not sleep. All these different thoughts were racing through my mind. I was thinking about so many different things. My friend's murder made me think about my own life as well. I saw how easy it was to be here on this planet one minute and gone in the next.

These thoughts haunted me and wouldn't leave. I took sleeping pills so I could sleep. I was still wide awake after an hour of lying in bed. I usually don't resort to alcohol, but that night I did. After two more hours, I thought that taking more sleeping pills wouldn't hurt me. Unfortunately, I had forgotten what amount I took earlier. I ended up overdosing.

Luckily, I was found in time and an ambulance was called. They thought I tried to commit suicide. That was not my intentions. I just wanted to sleep. I wanted all my thoughts to go away. I wanted the pain from my best friend being murdered to just go away. The hospital sent in a counselor and they wouldn't let me leave until they were convinced that I wasn't going to harm myself. That was a very humiliating experience to be looked at in this way.

Although at the time I was not happy with that experience, it taught me how to handle depression better. I learned that it's not good to run from things that are depressing me. I learned that it's better to deal with it instead of suppressing it. I also learned that if I'm not comfortable talking to anyone around me about things that are depressing me, that it's ok to talk to a therapist if I need to get it out.

Usually, it's therapeutic for me to write, sing or entertain to get things out. This experience changed my entire outlook on what depression is and how to deal with it. This leads me into introducing this chapter of Depression. These poems express Depression from different perspectives. It looks at different ways that Depression has been felt and dealt with. Welcome to the land of Depression.

Dark History

I cried and I cried
Not knowing what tomorrow will bring
If it's going to be the same as my past
Then I don't know if I can let that be

I'm just trying to survive
In this world that loves to hurt
It's almost like people get a high
Off of punishing when you don't deserve

It's no way to escape judgement
My past perception is still here today
It's like every time I turn around
My depression just won't shake

I've lost so many people I love
My world feels so alone
It's hard to know who to trust
When new people come into my home

I don't want to live my life in regret

I'm on this sinking ship

I'm trying to find a way out of it

But happiness keeps giving me the slip

I'm faced with my dark history

It's filled with hurt and pain

Can I be saved from my misery?

I can't believe I feel like this, I'm so ashamed

__Overdose__

What is going on?
Where am I?
I woke up and I'm in a hospital bed
And there are bandages around my head
I have no memory of what has happened
I'm a little loss and confused
And then I started to remember
I was at home in my bedroom

My analyzing was going too deep
Too many thoughts were in my head
I was laying there and I couldn't fall asleep
So I grabbed some sleeping pills instead
I leaned back and I could see the ceiling
I closed my eyes and I felt unrest
I rolled over and turned to the side
I held a pillow to my chest

All of a sudden I was feeling down
My thoughts were making me depressed
What has happened to my life?
I'm started to feel regret

After an hour passed by

I still couldn't sleep

I could see the sleeping pills

They were right next to me

If I took one more, what would it hurt?

It slipped my mind that earlier I was drunk

I calculated that I only took two

By the time I was done, I definitely had misused

I could only think of escaping

Why can't I just sleep?

I didn't want to think anymore

My thoughts kept haunting me

What can I do?

I need these thoughts out of my head

It just kept getting worst

All this anxiety ignited my plan

I was determined to sleep

I could take no more

I took more pills

Hoping it would make me snore

Finally I drifted into dreamland
I was flying in the clouds
I could see myself landing softly on the ground
There was a lot of laughter and people around
This was paradise, I couldn't ask for more
Suddenly, everything disappeared
This world was gone
I remember it fading away, even the sun

And now this nurse was right in my face
She said, wake up now, Are you ok?
I said what happened, why am I here?
She told me I was found at the top of my stairs
I wasn't breathing and I was passed out
There were pills next to me
It was an overdose
There was no doubt

Down

This feeling of sadness hits me deep
The waves are so hard, it's making me weep
I should be happy with all these people around me
But yet inside of this crowd, I still feel lonely

I'm going through the motions as I give them a smile
This same routine goes on day after day
Inside of me, I feel like giving a frown
Regardless of this, I still walk through town

I can't explain why I'm feeling this way
What can I do to make this feeling shake?
I'm trying to figure out while time is passing by
I want to get better, I'm ready to try

This feeling down feeling is so exhausting
There must be an end in sight
Will it finally leave me?
Will I ever have peace of mind?

Medication

I thought I was the only person
That experienced being depressed
But I see all these TV commercials
They have the prescriptions for it

It must be real popular
For people to feel down
Companies sell these feel happy drugs to millions
It's like a legal way to get stoned

Isn't depression a part of life?
Has every single person felt it?
These commercials make it seem so wrong
They want to cure it with medicine

Usually when I get depressed
I'm only down for a day or two
So in a situation like mine
Do I need medication too?

Another Hard Day

Another hard day to wake up to
Is everything still the same?
It's hard to see myself making it through
Will anything ever change?

As time and time pass on
Will I ever get stronger?
I can't stay stuck like this
My depressed days are getting longer

I don't know what will satisfy me
What more can I do?
I'm trying to put everything behind me
I feel like I always lose

So here's a toast
To another hard day
Maybe I will snap out of it
Maybe one day I will leave my cave

Feelings Of Vanity

Feelings of vanity enter into my thoughts
Hopelessness intrudes onto my spirit
Visions of despair crosses my mind
The aura of regression enters my soul
As I think about these thoughts of vanity
How will my life pan out before me?

I begin to wonder
Why am I here?
What is my purpose?
I need a reason to live
Will I ever find that answer?
I'm afraid I won't, this is my fear

Tears roll down my eyes
I cry from the lack of knowing
I search and search within
Where's the answer from my subconscious
I search for a reason to not give in
Will it be my season to dream again?

I'm searching and searching
The solution keep evading me
I get intense inside with frustration
Is this the way it has to be?
Is there a light at the end of this tunnel?
If there is, I'm blocked and I can't see

I hope I don't give up
The other side is waving with its hand
I'm trying to persevere but it's rough
This is my circumstance
I need some air to breathe
I need a fighting chance

I know everyone has obstacles
We all experience pain
But my life just seem so hopeless
This fact just keeps coming up again
Is this the course of my destiny?
These feelings of vanity appear

I Am So Unhappy Right Now

I am so unhappy right now

Tears are rolling inside my mind

And pouring out of my eyes

It soaks my face

I want more out of my life

But I don't know how to achieve it

I've lost my faith and my drive

It's like nothing is important to me in life anymore

I don't trust my friends

I'm not alone but I feel alone

I'm in this battle by myself

What must I do or say

To stop feeling this way

I'm looking for an answer in the wrong places

And I'm putting my time with the wrong faces

I've wasted so many years of my life

And now I have no passion

I have no will

It's like I just don't care about anything anymore

Why does life matter?

My brain is full of chatter

I'm sinking under

As I fill myself up with wonder

I'm questioning everything

When will I wake up?

Will I ever see the light of day?

I just feel so numb right now

And just don't care about anything

I'm so unhappy

If the average person looked at me

They would be amazed at my achievements

They would be shocked that I feel this way

Help Me

Right now, I feel so much pain
Why invest time into people?
Just to have a response that's in vain
I feel nothing right now

I feel like I have no purpose
Like I'm just passing time away
What am I working for?
Why put all this effort into life?

I only receive double pain
What am I fighting for?
Why am I here?
My state of mind is so clouded

I just want to enjoy life
Not saying I haven't before
I don't know how to get back to that
Can you help me?

Here I Am Again

It's been some time since I last saw you
Right now, I feel brand new
I wonder if I've lost the magic touch
The one that separates, the fake from the luck

I'm not sure if my life will have the qualities
That will surpass or even equal my reality
I've been through so much
I feel like I'm in a rut

It's like being a rat that's trapped in a maze
How long will I be at this stage?
At this point, will I ever know?
Will that answer be a yes or a no?

I try to breathe my reason
So that I overlook my vanity
I try to think of good seasons
I try to maintain an outside smile

So I'll keep moving on

Not knowing if I'm weak or strong

I get scared like everyone else

Where is my strength?

So here I am again

I'm back at your door

Depression, you're not my friend

Why do I keep coming back for more?

How Long?

I cried inside, as I live my life
How much pain must I bare?
When will my prize arrive?
I just don't know if I'll make it

My will inside is breaking
I'm yearning for a change
I need a break through today
I must find a way

I won't let my journey stop my fire
Is my lesson learned killing my desire?
Why is my reach for breakthrough bringing me down?
I must find a way to smile through my frown

My soul is losing its connection
I feel like I'm back at square one
How do I find encouragement?
When I feel so done

I just can't see past tomorrow

When today, I'm faced with sorrow

So I surrender just to find

That time isn't on my side

Chapter 5
What Does Life Mean?

Do you ever wonder what life means? Why are here? I have asked myself some of these questions before. What is my path? Where am I going? I don't believe there is a right or wrong answer to these questions. Some things in life are in our control and some things are not. And sometimes we make plans to have our life one way and we end up going a different direction.

At one point of time in my life, I planned on being an attorney. These were my thoughts when I was a teenager. I never would have imagined myself having a career as a writer or entertainer.

When I think about the meaning of life, it is extremely complex but yet so simple. I believe our meaning of life is what we individually define it. Some people find it through their faith or religion; others find meaning in other ways. I don't believe that one definition applies to every person. It shocks me to see the amount of controversy that the meaning of life has created over the centuries. It is also amazing to see people come together over common causes as well.

This chapter is a perfect close to this book. The collection of poems in this chapter reflects different outlooks on the meaning of life. It is from a thought provoking perspective.

Thoughts On A Cold Day

Today is a cold day
Outside it's ten degrees
The wind is blowing softly
It touches me with its chilly breeze

I'm walking outside by the docks
My mind is visualizing past thoughts
Their surfacing up one by one
Some of my memories are not clear

It's like an endless ocean of water
I want to remember my childhood years
I want to remember how it all started
I wonder if life has real meaning

But I'm not sure how much I need it
I've heard that time will always tell
Should I give up on searching for its meaning?
 Should I embrace vanity as well?

This Throbbing Headache

Ever since Wednesday, I've had a bad headache
It's so hard to describe this terrible pain
It's like someone took a wrench and pounded my head
I just need to sleep this off instead

It's so hard for someone else to understand
Unless they've experienced this pain like I had
I can't even look at the television screen
The light hits my eyes like a blinding beam

The will power to do anything entertaining is gone
This headache has me feeling like everything is wrong
What can I do to make it stop?
I'm tired of taking medicine that I get from the food shop

I don't want to get hooked on these over the counter drugs
It's got to be a way to make this pain unplug
I don't think I ever experienced this much pain in my life
This pain won't even let up at night

I'm trying to think of what could have caused this migraine
Was it the stress I went through earlier when it rained?
I tried to vent and let my troubles out
I talked about it over and over with my mouth

Is there something that I'm holding on to within?
This pain is a battle that I simply can't win
I don't understand, what else can I do?
I just want it to go away, this is the truth

I'm going to miss the party for New Year's Eve
With this throbbing headache, it's so hard to see
Why is this happening? Why now?
Am I supposed to be learning a lesson somehow?

Is there a way to make this a normal headache?
When it's a migraine, the pain punches me in the face
While it exist, my life will never be the same
This throbbing headache is just so strange

The True Purpose Of Life

Let us think

What is the purpose of life?

Why are we really here?

If we think about it, the answers are unclear

The future seems endless

As time seems to have no beginning

It's like a giant maze

Life seems to be a never-ending phrase

Is life really what we think it is?

A future filled with love and happiness

Seeing the understanding go asunder

My thoughts seem to dim and plunder

What is our real purpose here?

Like a black void it seems to not appear

For everything seems as if it's nothing

Even death seems silly to fear

As these thoughts of vanity cross my mind
I try to think of the deep meaning of it all
And I begin to realize
That everything in time will pass

All the things that mean so much to us
I think about reality, it doesn't mean that much
For those things lose their meaning
When time gets too rough

The purpose of this saying
Is not to send you into a woo
It's here to enlighten your mind's craving
The true meaning of life is within you

This Little Mouse

This little mouse
Ran all through my house
With its rugged skin
And big long head
The mouse just wants to have a home
He really doesn't want to bother anyone
He hides himself from everyone else
The reason is because he will be treated unfair
The house won't receive him with open arms
They'll kick him out and say leave us alone

This little mouse have feelings too
He doesn't know where else to go
He doesn't know what to do
He just wants a home and some food
Are we like this mouse?
Have you ever been unwelcomed somewhere?
What about a situation in which no one cares?
I've felt like this mouse before.
Have you?

The Serene Amazement

Quietly the serene moment appears
Thoroughly engaging in absolute purity
As the contemplation begins inside
There is a certain mood that settles

What a peaceful thing to see
Those collections that resides in abstract
As the maze is put through the test
The resolute amazement comes at last

What is the definition of this serenity?
What is the resolution of infinity?
For whomsoever shall guess
That soul will be as a heavenly body

Oh the colorful serenity appears
What an amazing thing
I'm filled inside with tranquillity for years
This moment is beyond my eyes

The Three Realities

As I collect my thoughts, I reflect on our meeting
I think about all the descriptions
That one could prescribe
And I see three different realities
Please be patient, as I explain them to thee

In one world I see a hard-core warrior
One that places his shield on his breast
He covers the doorway to his heart
And that warrior places a helmet on his mind
To block anyone from possessing his thoughts
But that same warrior has a softer side
One in which he secretly takes pride
And really, his compassion matches his strength
His yearn for love reflects what his past actions mean
For I wonder if this warrior is afraid to be alone

In another world I see a war within
I hear the battle cry as the pain caves in
The first army represents the world of solitude
Fighting for the soul and the mind too
For if this army wins, the soul shall never love again

The second army is definitely a challenge
They are fighting for the hopeless romantic
This soul has a lot of love to give
It's hard to say which will win
They both have powerful weapons and cleverness within
This war has been long lasting
Who knows who will come out on top?
It will definitely be surprising

And in the third world I see a body with two heads
One is a child and one is a man
The child is afraid to venture on his own
Fearing if he should call a new place home
And the man is consistently knocking the child's head
As he say, dear child, grow up and be a man
Take a chance on depending on yourself
And be grateful that you have good health
For no matter what decision is made
The man will always be a child
And the child will always be a man
They are two personalities within the same one

I know that these three worlds may be confusing

But if you look at the stars, the meaning will be useful

For you will understand what really is going on

As you read about the different realities

For every story won't have a rhythm or rhyme

But the message will arrive just in time

Uncertainty

There's a certain uncertainty

That comes within my soul

I try to be brave

But it's hard to stay bold

I think about my future each and every day

I try to work on my goals

Without procrastination hindering my way

It just seems very difficult at times

It seems as if all open doors

Eventually will close

It seems like life just taunts me

It gives me promises

And in return it delivers problems

What must I do to survive?

What must I do to succeed?

How much do I have to sacrifice?

I already gave up friends and family

I just don't understand

The things that are before me

For when I ask a higher power

The answer is uncertainty

Want More

Why do we want more?
Is it hard to be content?
It's something about desire
That makes you feel like you've missed

It's hard to find balance
Is it wrong to set goals?
When do we have to settle?
How will we really know?

Personally, I can't sit still
I always have to work
It's the passion that lies within
If I suffocate it, I will go berserk

I'm not saying there's anything wrong
For those who choose to be the opposite
Maybe we have to customize how we are
Our personalities will determine which

The Real Possession

The tiresome body appears

As thoughts of a home linger

The never-ending search seems hopeful

For that special place where peace resides

As the circle of time revitalizes

Having such simplicity as a child

The round motion continues

Seeming to never end

Wonderment and amazement is born

As these comfortable moments are envisioned

Time will create peace within

So as these memoirs of thinking comprehends

The innermost desires of the heart

I see the path to the future closing in

It doesn't seem like it's too far

As the curve infested journey

Continues past the end

I see that the real place of possession

Is in the heart and mind within

The Foolish Deceiver

Why do you think that I'm a fool?
You truly believe that your deception rules
Your ultimate goal is positive regression
For if anyone around you has achievements
You view this as worldly aggression
Stop blaming other races
Stop blaming other people

If you only release your positive energy
And kill your spirit of being lazy
Then you will see things change
For the better and not the worst
You will see closed doors open
You will see blindness turn to vision
But instead of taking the road less travelled
You choose to take the path of deception

Do you wonder why sadness comes your way?
Think about the saying
For every action, there are consequences
For all of life's bills, you will have to pay

So take heed to this instruction

Start releasing qualities

That you expect from others

And then you'll finally see

Your dreams come true

Stop being that ultimate fool

By thinking your deception rules

A New Era

A new era has crept on my soul
As I try to hold on to things I knew
My mind began to see new dreams
That hasn't materialized into reality

For I wonder where will my life be
When ten years have left me
On some days, I see no vision
On others, the sight is so clear

One interesting fact that has appeared
Is that the journey can mean more than the end
The path can be enjoyed much more than the final destination
Wisdom is born with this experience

I've learned that life can be simple
Like a bird that flies around in the sky
While enjoying the flight of the path
They continue to stay focused on their prey

From this day forward

I will view life in a simple way

I will keep my mind free

While achieving the meaning of my life destiny

The Lesson From The Fishermen

Patience, patience, patience
This is a true virtue
I thought about the word patience
When I saw the fishermen, in pairs of two

They waited real patiently until they caught their prey
We can learn a lot from this view
This reminds me to think about my goals and dreams
I think about how far away it seems

But when the thought of patience
Entered into my contemplation
I realized that every dream takes time
It takes work to make realization

But how do we accomplish this reality?
How do we make our dreams come true?
How does this virtue reveal the truth?
I think patience teaches us wisdom

With all of these thoughts, comes knowledge
If I wish to achieve my dreams
Then I must start today by planting a seed
I will chip away at my dreams

One by one, day by day
This helps me keep procrastination away
I will keep laziness out of my space
I will start taking steps, one by one

And add a little patience along with some fun
This is what the fishermen do
When they're teaching us about this priceless virtue
This experience requires discipline to achieve

Just remember the truth about patience
It's not to be confused with laziness
For patience equals persistence
And with persistence we overcome resistance

The amazement is great in my view
As I watch the fishermen in pairs of two

Conclusion

Our voyage on the destiny of life train has come to an end. We have explored the different mountains and valleys of this complex word called Life. We took a look at overcoming obstacles through "Turning Lemons to Lemonade." We even ventured into the world of being "Ticked Off." Then we drifted on to the island of "Letting Life Flow." After we left the island, we explored the land of "Depression." And the last stop on this train was "What Does Life Mean?"

As we took the voyage, you experienced different highs and lows of emotions. This is a reflection of how life is. One concluding point that I will leave you with is, "Life is what you make it." Some situations are predicated upon how you manage your reaction. Other situations require you to take action. We will now exit the train of "Life Destiny."

Steve Ryan is the author of "Life Destiny." Be sure to check out his other books. Visit him on the web at www.SteveRyan.com

www.ingramcontent.com/pod-product-compliance
Lightning Source LLC
Chambersburg PA
CBHW071307040426
42444CB00009B/1901